The scientific economic paper: from writing to publishing

Mihai Mutascu

To Anne-Marie and my parents

Contents

Preamble

This book has been written by a non-native English speaker. It is addressed especially to the young researchers, debutants, devoted to the economic research (e.g. master students, Ph.D. students, post-doc students and young researchers) and also anyone in the academic environment and not only.

The volume is not exclusively a scientific one, being more appropriate to a friendly short 'story' about how to write and publish a scientific economic paper.

The idea of this tale has origins in my publishing international experience with the worldwide recognized publishers (e.g. Emerald, Elsevier, Sage, Springer, Taylor & Francis, Wiley).

Unfortunately, the rigors of such publishers cannot be experienced through the research training during the academic period.

Thus, many ideas and reflections in this book are results of my personal publishing experience, but also the vector of dozens of feed-backs received from colleagues in my country or abroad. A good experience in publishing I also gained, starting with 2011, as editor-in-chief of the scientific international journal "Economic Research Guardian".

The content of the book I propose is relayed on a legitimate question, that looking back in time, I have asked myself, being preoccupied by the subject: how to write and publish a good scientific economic paper? I thought that the right answer must to be sequential, starting from the identification of topic to the final stage of paper publishing, running the all related gauntlets.

Without discouraging anyone, even if there is a strong theoretical and empirical ground, a publishing in a top international journal can take in average between 2 and 3 years (1 year in the best case!) or can be doomed to failure irremediably at this level of rigours. In the last undesirable situation, in order to preserve the results of research, the quality standard of the journals must be gradually diminished.

Finally, I hope the lecture will not bore you and my stories, presented at the second-person singular, about how to write and publish a scientific economic paper, will be very useful in your scientific career.

Mihai Mutascu,

March 13, 2017

Introduction

There is no doubt on the importance of scientific publications in ones academic career, as the main condition to apply for an academic position is the scientific quality of the applicant's papers.

The negotiation of an academic position and its remuneration has as main argument the scientific visibility of the candidate, especially at the international level, not only the teaching skills. Any reputable academic institution analyses an application also from the perspective of the potential advantages offered by the recruiting candidate: the international collaborations, the experience in organizing conferences, the editorial background, the research capacity to coagulate a research team etc.

Briefly, we talk about the scientific prestige! For example, Princeton University is celebre through its eminent graduates and also through Albert Einstein who served there for a couple of years but not as a teacher, but as a brilliant researcher. Per a contrario, he seemed to be catastrophic in teaching. In the same university, similar, we can mention the case of Nobel prised laureate in Economy from 1994, for the games theory, John Forbes Nash.

Even if many voices blame and try to minimize the role of scientific research, for a major part of academic institutions from abroad, the research plays a crucial role in the live of those academic communities. The main idea is that the research results can be included in the class courses and practice seminars, offering the students all news vanguard scientific discovers in the field.

The publishing of very good papers is not a process exclusively related to the researcher's skills, but also to publishing type of strategy. Without a coherent publishing strategy, many times, despite the intensive work consumed, the results are expected to appear or, if these findings appear, they are modest. More dangerous is that such failures will have a 'boomerang' effects on the long term, having adverse effects on the researcher's moral, especially on the young generations. In many cases, persons with excellent research perspectives will succumb and will follow completely different career directions.

Even if many publishing strategies must be 'stolen' during the career or are achieved through personal experience, it is recommended not neglecting the books or articles which offer ideas and advices in this strategic area.

About topic and title

When you decide to research and publish in the economic area, the first dilemma you have that is related to the topic should be investigated and to the most appropriate title. You want your manuscript to be very good received by the readers, but, at the same time, you try also to maximize the chance for publishing in prestigious journals. Try to avoid following your own impressions such as 'I know it better' because you often may be wrong.

The topic

Many time the topic is a compromise born either from the desire to have a quantitative publishing visibility, as your CV to become impressive, or from the 'restrictions' imposed by context (i.e. the obsessive request of your PhD director, the research grant you are involved in, the coordinates suggested by your post-doc supervisor, the research strategy of your university etc.)

In the first case, the fever of numerous publication is a general characteristic of educational and research systems where the academic positions are held based on quantitative criteria, with excellent effects on short term. But on long term, the publishing bulimia (usually consisting in poor quality papers resulted from the high density of papers on a short period of time) is evil and impossible to be corrected in the future. The marks remained in your CV are irreversible and the accession to good opportunities during your career will receive the appellative 'impossible'.

In the second case, the limitations given by context are a bad necessity with which you should get habituated and resigned.

Still, if you are able to deal with the above two challenges, choosing a good working topic implies knowing several small tips.

The first tip is to identify the recent economic literature pulse, as it results from published papers in the famous journals in the field. It is unanimously accepted that such top journals exist. In this way, different international rankings are offered by various international organisms (e.g. Thomson Reuters), governmental agencies (e.g. AERES or CNRS in France, UEFISCDI in Romania) or even research institutes (e.g. Tinbergen Institute).

Reading "a la long" the content of those journals, you can easily identify your preferred research domain within the 'trend' of the moment. Avoid here to count obscure publishers and focus on the famous ones: Berkeley Electronic Press, Cambridge University Press, Elsevier, Emerald, Harvard University Press, MIT Press, Oxford University Press, Princeton University Press, Routledge, Sage, Springer, Taylor & Francis, Wiley-Blackwell, Yale University Press etc.

Each attempt to get out of these canons can generate unwanted falls. Think about! It is difficult to imagine that you will make a 'new market segment' (i.e. a new topic), especially when you are at the beginning of your career and/or your affiliated institution is not so known, not to say anonymous. Yes, the miracle exists, but not so often!

The second tip is to follow the titles of the papers presented at conferences, symposiums, workshops, lectures, laboratory seminars or at other similar scientific meetings for dissemination of the research results. You can obtain important information about publishing 'trend' as a major part of scientific communications will be finally published. All aspects you identify during these events are strongly connected with published papers in big journals, their presentation being a normal step before publication. As a consequence, you should pay a special attention to attend such meetings as well as to the criteria for selecting them. Avoid as possible you can to attend: multi- and ultra-disciplinary meetings; conferences with very high fees and extended social programmes; conferences which propose publications on CD or by proceeding type with different indexing forms; meetings with anonymous keynote speakers, exclusive national board members or modest publishing status members (i.e. you can see their professional probity by checking the list of publications on the internet and by identifying whether the published papers fall into the above mentioned categories); and also those organized by obscure institutions or by organism which manage in the same time many conferences from various research domains. Even if you do not present a paper but attend the meetings, focus on the conferences organised by celebre universities (i.e. consult in this case the multitude of international rankings) and by the recognized organisms or research associations (e.g. American Economic Association, American Marketing Association, International Atlantic Economic Association, International Institute of Public Finance, Public Choice Society, Royal Economic Society etc.).

The third tip is to exploit the research tool and methods novelty (i.e. I refer here especially to the econometrics and mathematic modelling). Your chances for publishing can be increased step-by-step if, although your topic is well exploited, you add new results, obtained with cutting-edge research tools. But in this case you need to have a very good control of econometrics and mathematic modelling and also to have a good knowledge of advanced econometrics and statistics software (e.g. Matlab, R, STATA, EViews, Gauss, Gretl, Rats, TSP, SPSS etc.). The novelty in term of research tools should be 'inspired' from the top journals in the field (e.g. Econometrica, Econometric Theory, Journal of Econometrics, Econometric Reviews etc.) and transformed into the software language code.

The fourth tip is connected with the previous one. It means the 'borrowing' in the research economic area of tools specific to other research domains. In this situation, there is only one problem you confront: the editor scepticism or, more certain, his conservatism. Practically, the idea is to focus on ultra-exploited topics but to use the tools and methods which are specific to the other research domains. For example, in the last years, in the economic research area gain more territory the methods from frequency domain modelling or the approaches which combine both time and frequency, such as the wavelet. The wavelet was developed by Morlet and Grossmann during '80 and it is specific to domains such as geophysics, image processing, medicine, astronomy etc.

The fifth tip is to localize and exploit the main national and international economic tendencies, with their given amplitude and complexity which exceeds the normal coordinates (e.g. eurozone crisis, Greece crisis, the crisis of public debts etc.). Not at least, you should pay a special attention to the geopolitical context (e.g. the migration phenomenon in the last years in Europe, the wars from Arab word, the conflict in

Ukraine, the secession pressure in Quebec, Catalonia and Scotland and so on). Each of the previous examples suggest a good topic to be followed. Most of them are also reflected in the written and audio-visual mass media.

The sixth tip is to adapt your research topic according to different national and international research strategies. Without any doubt, such a tip cannot be taken as rule. Generally speaking, each country has its particular research strategy, which includes very well individualised and defined topics. Moreover, such research strategies are found also at international level, being performed by different international organisms and agencies. For example, in the last years, the topics such as 'ecological economics' or 'energy economics' are demanded and appreciated.

The last tip, the seventh, is to appeal for an 'exotic' or 'taboo' item in your chosen research domain. In this case, irrespective of the selected investigation tool or without considering the normal domain 'trend', your publishing chances increase as your results are more controversial and sustained by good empirical results. The empirical ground is very important for your study and paper credibility.

Such topics are the public audience delights but do not provide you a high number of citations in the international recognised journals (e.g. the lipstick consumption and economic growth, the bourse quotes and climatic conditions, the Moon phases and economic behaviour etc.).

The title

The paper's title is the consequence of the chosen topic and it is required to suggest in few words the essence of your research. Similar to the choose of the topic, there is also a series of tips which should be considered when you decide the final form of the title.

A special attention deserves the so called "running title" or "head title", more precisely the "short title". These titles are often required by many publishers, appear in parallel with the normal ones and consist of 3-5 words (usually, include the paper's keywords). The 'running title steams from the necessity of reader guidance, facilitating the using of 'RSS feeds'. For publishers and indexed databases, the short titles increase also the efficiency in managing electronic paper archives. Usually, the 'running title' appears centred in the top of the page, on each of paper's pages together with the name of the author.

Coming back, the first tip to identify the main title is the rule of length. The most 'efficient' title must be short, not more 7-8 words. It is required to suggestively capture, in few words, the central idea of research. This rule can be disregarded only in special situations, generally when a short title cannot fully capture the essence of the paper.

The second tip is the clarity of expression. Be pragmatic. Do not use 'pretentious' or 'pompous' words. Make this only if the research requires such needs. Be clear and concise, by using a combination of words able to coagulate a part of elements. Further, these can easily be considered as keywords.

An alembicated title is the 'right' way to the rejection of the paper. This will be the decision given by any respected journals.

The third tip is related to the specification of the subject or investigated subjects (attention, here is not the case of topic!). Usually, the subjects are represented by a group of countries, an individual country, economic branches and sectors, companies, households or various categories of individuals. The rule is to indicate, either in the beginning of the title, or in its end, the targeted subject of analysis (e.g. "The Austrian touristic sector: a study about hotel investments" or "A study about saving in Germany"). Usually, is used the syntagma "The case of the sector X". The tip of 'targeted subject' can also have negative reverse effect as it can selectively capture the attention of readers.

The fourth tip is to include the name of the method used in the empirical part. Usually, it is recommended to insert the name of method in the paper title only if it is complex or cutting edge. It does not make sense to announce with 'the red carpet', from right the title, a banal method used in the empirical part. The idea is to capture the attention of the reader through the name of method which, if it is absolutely a new one, will give a plus of interest.

The fifth tip is to specify the period of investigation. Most often, a special interest have different horizons of time which are related to various events or economic trends. Additionally, the time period missing from the title can generate a dilution of interest for readers, who will give up to identify the analysed period, often as lack of time.

The sixth notable tip is to use the interrogative construction form. The title as 'interrogation' represents a particular form. Irrespective of the topic, it will capture the attention of readers, as the lecturer will try to find the response at the question proposed by author. In this case, it is required to be sure you are available to offer it!

The seventh tip is represented by the exclamatory construction form of the title, which should denote a 'discovered fact', without any doubt, including all the paper conclusions. This case deserves a special attention! Captured by title, your readers will look for strong demonstrations for your findings. You are free to appeal such titles when you are absolutely sure on your reasoning and demonstrations.

Finally, the eighth tip is correlated with the 'exoticism' topic and represents, obviously, its consequence. Certainly, if you want to chose a topic considered by major part of researcher as 'exotic' or 'taboo', it is required to be reflected in your paper title. Bluntly, declare this exotic aspect through adequate words. Also, it will be very opportune to highlighted them by using the quotation marks.

Do not forget that your title is not 'nailed' and any improvements are more than welcomed, especially when the suggestions of corrections come from editors and/or reviewers.

***

Without pretending to be rules, all these tips and suggestions, both for chosen topic and title, will increase your international research visibility and also will help you to maximise the chances to publish in good journals.

Paper length

After you clarified the topic and defined the paper title, the next challenge is the length of the paper. All right, but you will tell me that you have no idea how to intuit the vastness of the research. I agree with you, but firstly you must have a good knowledge of the general framework of scientific papers typology.

The top world journals accept for review in order to be published many manuscripts, with a wide typological forms, concisely declared in the journal's mission. Mainly, in the economic research area, you can have contact with the different categories of papers: the note, the research article, the comment, the review, the preliminary results and the erratum.

1/ The note or short-paper is a form of paper characterized by short length, usually without exceeding 6-7 pages total (at several publishers are excepted the annexes and appendix). In the case of such papers, the density of ideas on page is very high, being recommended pragmatism and clarity in writing. Under any circumstances do not try to exceed the page threshold imposed by publisher as the rejection of your paper will be imminent!

2/ The research article is the classical form of a paper, which has around 7-8 pages, rarely it might exceed 25-28 pages (exclusive, the annexe and appendix). Often, the optimal paper length is suggested by the publisher and must be 'sacredly' respected! Do not try to force the rule because you have all chances for the paper to be rejected. In the best scenario, you will receive a second and last chance, you being ask to recalibrate your manuscript according to the journal's criteria. Certainly, each scientific paper can be recalibrated also to become a note. In this situation, the adjustments must not affect the essence of research conclusions.

3/ The comment is a very short paper, not exceeding 2-3 pages, generally without a good individualized structure, which has as main particularity the fact that the authors comment a paper already published by other authors. Many times, the comments represent the critics of the results, at which, sometime, the author of the comment suggest solutions for improving the paper or even new research directions.

4/ The review or survey is a paper form with a length between 10-15 pages, including also the list of references. This type of paper summarises and reviews the literature in the field related to a specify topic, highlighting the main directions of thought and the theoretical breaking points. Obviously, the review is based on papers already published and does not aim to offer new results or new research methods. It is recommended to approach such manuscripts a little bit later, when you already have a minimal publishing experience. Practically, after a routine consumed with research articles, you can focus on the papers by review type. Do not forget that some journals publish exclusively only the reviews, in this named case review journals.

The review is a type of paper which deserves a huge capacity of synthesis and an extended professional experience.

5/ The preliminary result is a sort of paper similar with the note in terms of length, for which the main scope is more a disseminative one, to announce the preliminary results obtained. The major part of preliminary results will become research papers after validation and finalization of the results. Additionally, from a copyright perspective, this type of paper allows the author to protect his ideas and preliminary research results.

6/ The erratum represents a pseudo-form of paper, usually not exceeding 2-3 pages, where the author or editor makes corrections or offers additional explanations regarding a paper already published in the same journal. The errata can be written either when the author found that results are not valid or needs additional details, or the editor considers, many times at the readers notice, the need of several adjustments which are not the author's fault.

Besides these categories of papers, the big international journals practice other two forms of papers, which in essence are research articles but with particular names. These names are given by the way of recruiting papers for publication. We can individualise: the special issue paper and invited paper.

The special issue paper is a paper published in a special journal issue, which is not necessary counted officially within the volumes or issues of the journal, being the result of a conference, symposium or any other scientific events. Usually, the manuscripts are selected by the editor or invited editor during the paper presentations. They invite the authors to submit their papers after the event. The review of these papers is a little bit more 'lax' comparative with the regular one.

The invited paper is an ordinarily published paper but the submission of the manuscript for review is made at the express of the invitation editor. Please note that it does not exist any 'special treatment' during the review, all such papers being reviewed as the regular classical ones.

Now, you are very well informed regarding the length of a paper, given aforementioned typology. I am sure that you try to find another response: which of the considered types of papers will be more appropriate for you?

Certainly, all types are good but the research article and review can be particularly evidenced in this pallet of forms. The comment has a good valence especially if the targeted paper belongs to a famous researcher or is published in a top journal. As advise, at the beginning of your academic career is quite opportune to follow the preliminary results or notes. As soon as you gains more experience, you can target also the research article.

At the maturity of publishing, when you already have published a consistent number of research articles, you can consider that is time to 'attack' the review and comment. All these coordinates are in reality suggestions, which do not intend to be rules, but appear as logical things from a strategic point of view. Certainly, there is not any barrier to try to publish reviews or comments since the beginning of your professional career.

Writing

The effective writing of a paper is the most important part of a researcher's career, who has already accumulated a reasonable theoretical and methodological expertise. The paper publishing in a top journal is suitable only under such auspices. Whatever, some victories can also be won out of this context, but they denote you was under a circumstantial favourable context (with other words, you are a luck person!) or the journal is an insignificant one related to the 'select' world of economic research environment. Be careful! It is not to your advantage to have a CV filled with obscure publications, many of them belonging to other research domains. You should note that, at international level, there is a recognized and very well delimitated group of top journals, several of them not being indexed in the celebre ISI Thomson Reuters database.

Certainly, I suppose you are excited by two main questions, when you think at the effective writing: how to fix the structure of the paper and which are the main coordinates of its content? Certainly, in both situations it does not exist a general prescription but, as the major parts of papers are research articles, I will exclusively refer to this category. Finally, several details will be offered also for the rest of paper categories.

The structure

Determining the paper configuration is the first step which should be followed when you decide to propose and publish your research results. In some countries, the 'old' economics school suggests the following of extended and complex structure, where you insert the many and many concepts, definitions, classifications and enumerations. The theory of 'nothing'! If you follow this way, you are completely wrong and your publishing chances are practically zero! Do you know why? Think a little bit! At least two explanations arise. The first one is connected to the minimal methodological requirements, while the second one represents an important strategic element.

In the last case, the editors, in order to ensure a unitary review, prefer written papers which follow a standard consecrated format, which can be easily identified by consulting few papers already published.

Therefore, without considering as a rule, the classical structure of a research paper in the economic domain has three parts:
- title page;
- the effective content, and
- the annexes and appendix.

1/ The title page is the first page of a paper, irrespective of typology, and includes: the title and/or running title, the name and surname of the author with affiliation, the abstract, the keywords and the JEL codes of the paper.

Some publishers also require short professional presentations of the author called 'highlights', (more precisely, the short sentences or phrases of approximately 4-6 sequentially posted). With these elements you will highlight the topic, the dataset used, the method followed, the main findings of research and the final principal conclusion. Usually, the 'highlights' replace the paper abstract.

Concretely, as we already discussed about the paper title, I am starting now the explanations regarding the other elements and also sections of the paper.

1a/ The name and surname, including the affiliations and professional addresses of the authors, must contain all the names of the persons who participated to the research and paper write, with their affiliations and related professional addresses.

Eh, and now we have the first main dilemma! Who is the first co-author? What will be the order should of the rest names?

Generally, the order of names is a custom related to the specificity of research domain but, in economy, we can unanimously accept the order according to the main contributions to research. The first author is regularly the one who collected the data and employed the estimations, followed by the one who wrote the literature review and, further, if is the case, by the co-author who performed the methodology part. The conclusion is the section where all the co-authors participate. The second presentation option, indeed rarely registered, reflects the order of co-authors based on the alphabetical criterion. Never ever arrange the co-author names relied on the age, academic position or administrative function! Although, such hierarchical arrangements are often registered in some countries, but disowned in the countries with recognized level of research, sometime being considered even ridicule.

The affiliations refer to the names of institutions or organisms where the authors currently activate or with which they have other types of academic relationship, as well as the contact addresses of these institutions. There is no problem if you use more than one affiliations, as in many cases the authors have both position of associated or visiting researcher. A very important aspect, do not forget to provide a valid email address, preferably the professional one. If the professional address is not available, for the correspondence with the editor, you can use an email address with a decent user name, which should comprise your name and surname.

1b/ The abstract is a component which follows the list of names and co-author affiliations. Its length should be no more than few sentences (the optimal level is around 9-10 rows) and should reflect:
- the targeted issue and its importance (i.e. the topic);

- the targeted objective, the analysis period and the investigation method;
- the main findings and the modality of how these outcomes are fixed or clarify the assumed issue and
- the main research conclusions.

Avoid as much as possible to insert in the abstract content numbers, references or mathematic formulas. Please note that there is also a so called 'extended abstract', which presents the paper as a short plan, on no more than 1 page. This type of abstract is generally the result of paper submission to conferences, symposiums or other similar scientific events.

As a rule, please consider that the abstract is the last written component of a paper, after you have finished all results and research conclusions.

1c/ The keywords include an array of 4-8 words or group of words, strongly related to the topic of research, which confers additional valence to the generated ideas or research results obtained. The words can be easily identified by topic, title and paper abstract. Essentially, the keywords have the mission to include in a 'short space' the essential elements pointed out during the paper, as 'large space'.

1d/ The JEL codes or JEL classification[1] are a frequent appearance in research articles in the economic domain and allow to identify the papers based on topic and research domain search. JEL is the acronym for Journal of Economic Literature. The JEL codes are the work of the American Economic Association and include letters and numbers. The letters denote the category, while the first and second numbers capture the research sub-categories (e.g. D62 - Externalities).

2/ The actual content is the most important part of a paper, having a particular structure depending on the paper's category, as it is a note, research article, comment, review, preliminary result or erratum. Given its importance, the effective content deserves a special attention. Therefore, a distinct sub-section has been assigned accordingly.

3/ The annexes and appendix finalise the paper and follow, generally, the effective content of paper, more precisely the section of references. Here, you can insert tables, figures, graphics and mathematic formulas, all numbered (i.e. usually with "A" before numbering, in order to suggest

---

[1] More details can be found at:
https://www.aeaweb.org/econlit/jelCodes.php

that the elements belong to annexes and appendix). It is mandatory to announce in the text all insertions !

In many cases, a section generically called the 'acknowledgements' interposes between the effective content and the annexes.

The acknowledgements denote 2-3 rows written by the author, in which he expresses the thanks to all persons who indirectly participated in the paper writing, mentioning also the names of those persons. Usually, the name order is established according to individual contributions to the paper improvement. The contributions refer to ideas, comments, observations, remarks, software codes etc. Here, in acknowledgements, the author can also assume that any mistakes or omissions belong his/herself exclusively. Some journals ask and post the acknowledgements even on the title page.

The effective content

The effective content is the core of the paper, as here is counted a large part of research work. If the text is in English, it is required to be short and clear in explanations, avoiding the very long phrases and alembicated sentences. You should pay a special attention to the different translations of notions and concepts, which in English often have consecrate forms (e.g. which in French is 'pression fiscale', in English is 'tax burden', no 'fiscal pressure', or which in French is 'politique fiscale', in English is 'tax policy', no 'fiscal policy').

As I already said, the effective content differs as the paper is a note, research article, comment, review, preliminary results or erratum.

The note, research article and preliminary results have more or less similar structure.

The content of note, research article and preliminary results

I reiterate the fact that the note, research article and preliminary results have relatively the same structure, the main differences generally arising from the paper's length. For simplification, I will describe the effective content for such types of papers with reference only to the research article.

Usually, the content of research article includes:

- the introduction;
- the literature;
- the data and methodology;
- the results, and
- the conclusions.

1/ The 'Introduction' is the first section of a research paper, in average no more than 2-4 pages.

The opening construction of the "Introduction" is called the 'catch up phrase' and has the main goal to announce the importance of the chosen topic, suggesting the readers the idea of investigation and the general research framework.

After that, a descriptive part will follow. Here, the main topic schools of thought are sequentially and analytically presented, highlighting also their recognized exponents. Without a reason do not introduce here definitions, banal and ultra-known concepts or branched classifications and characteristics.

Please note that it is not a big deal to use such explanations in a research article as the readers are very experimented in this case.

Moreover, avoid to use dashes in classifications and change them with other different forms of presentation. For example, you can use: (i), (ii), (iii)... or (a), (b), (c)... and so on.

Progressively, you can choose to follow what is so called the "funnel". This means that as much as you advance at the descriptive part, you should converge to the paper researched topic (i.e. you treat from general to specific). With other words, it is required to converge theoretically towards your topic.

After you fix the theoretical and descriptive component, the next stage is to emphasise the topic and the aim of your research, accentuating the targeted subjects and analysed period.

Do not forget to show why the targeted subject is an important aspect of the literature in the field and why is interesting to be investigated. As argument, you can use short context analyses, by performing synthetic indicators (preferably illustrated in tables and figures), as well as different official positions about the importance of the subject, assumed by various countries and international organisms.

Last but not least, you can exploit the references in the text, by invoking the names of recognized authors already having important contributions related to your topic and subject. The references in text usually appear in a standardised form, according to the journal's style where you want to disseminate you results (e.g. Taylor, 2011 or Buchanan (1986)).

Avoid as much as possible to use unfinished papers (working paper) or those presented at scientific events as reference sources, because this sort of papers do not have a recognized scientific status, the results being under validation. Separately, you also can use citations, by taking whole text body as they were written by the authors.

Attention! The use of citations must be temperate, it is mandatory to accompany the text body took over by the reference to paper's author names, year and page. In any circumstance, do not take over more than 1-3 sentences! You cannot use as citations whole phrases! Should you do this, irrespective of the quotation marks introduced, you can be accused of plagiarism. The citation has rather a demonstrative role and is employed when you do not want to alter the sense of original text.

The analysed period deserves to be also justified, in order to highlight why the chosen period of time is interesting for the study. Do not worry if you investigate an older period of time. You just have to give a pertinent explanation according to the general research framework where is related to your topic.

After this fragment, it is required to show the main conclusions obtained, specifying also the analysing tool used. Certainly, this part will be written at a later stage, as well as the abstract, more precisely after you finalized the results and conclusions.

At the end of section do not forget a crucial part: the main contributions of your paper to the literature in the field. State here which are the main contributions of the paper for the literature in the field by referring to the novelty of results, quality of data, the research methodologies followed and so on. If your paper does not offer anything new, than it is not an authentic research, being unsuitable for publishing.

The "Introduction" section should be ended with a short fragment of no more 1-2 sentences where is shortly explained the structure of the paper.

2/ The 'Literature' is chronologically the second section of a research article, following the 'Introduction' section.

This section is in fact the part of developing

theoretical and descriptive elements from 'Introduction', which you will widely and analytically reveal the main theoretical breakpoints from literature. Be prepared to offer here details about: the pioneer work in field, the main existing theories and its promoters, the importance of debates, the existing empirical studies and your expectances related to the researched topic and, why not, the main working hypotheses. Many authors deal with existing empirical studies by grouping them according to the targeted subjects and identified methods of analyse. Usually, in this cases, the scholars appeal at tabular form of presentations.

Separately, you can dedicate a special paragraphs to the literature regarding the targeted topic by following the same coordinates as the previous ones. It is very important to present you position related to the existing writes and targeted subject. As fewer papers are written, as better for you is, because you will be one of the first researchers which will approach, at incipient stage, the literature in filed.

3/ 'Data and methodology' represents a section with two sequences, which follows the literature: the first one is related to the data presentation, while the second one is reserved for the description of the methodology you chose.

The data should be concisely presented, insisting on the modalities of data collection. It is mandatory to explain, for each series: the reason of their selection, the name, unit of measurement, scale of intensity, period of time, frequency and the source of series. It is recommended to use data which are out of any doubt regarding the quality, provided by official agencies of statistics, international organisms or notorious companies in the field. Also, you should refer and present all added series adjustments, arguing the necessity of those interventions (e.g. modality of calculus, seasonal adjustments, trend corrections, normalizations etc.).

In many cases, the authors present also theoretically the methods used, if those have a higher level of complexity. At the beginning of this methodological part, specify the tested relationship. If there is some mathematical form, do not hesitate to present the equations which give sense of your model performed.

Here, do not forget to: indicate the method followed, argue why such a method is the most appropriate to your investigation and reveal the name of the author of method by inserting it as reference in text and also in the reference list. It is very important to emphasise why your method improves the quality of results by comparing with the existing classical tools.

In other words, you should highlight why your method is a superior tool to the existing one, usually used in the literature.

If you chose econometric estimations with control variables, do not forget to present those variables, to offer a description of details and, very important, to argue their selection. For explanation, you can appeal to the related literature in the field.

Next step is to reveal your intuitions regarding the results. More precisely, you have to show your position in respect to the expected results arisen from analysis, certainly, in strong connection with the literature (e.g. in the econometric analysis, specify the expected coefficient signs of variables).

4/ The 'Results' section practically transposes the previous section. Here are illustrated the main 'output' generated by your research.

In the first part, if you need to analyse the dataset, it is required to describe also the performed tests. More eloquent is to use tables, figures and graphics. Do not insert in the tables irrelevant information and offer all details needed for the readers to easily understand what you have done. Here, number all the tables, attach titles and do not forget to announce those tables in the body text. Below tables you can add 'notes' when you want to offer different explanations which help interpreting the results.

A very good example is the table below (Table 1):

Table 1: The results of the VIF test

Variables/test	VIF	1/VIF
GDP	4.05	0.247145
Payment balance	2.59	0.385561
Size of industrial sector	2.41	0.415257
Corruption index	2.21	0.451908
Inflation rate	1.17	0.858316
...	...	...
Mean VIF	2.05	

Note: the VIF denotes "variance inflation factor".

After the data analysis, you should start to present the effective results, where the generated overcomes will be described gradually. Here also utilize for better illustration tables, figures and graphics. After that, emphasise how your results confirm or not the literature findings. If there are interesting results, do not hesitate to additionally highlight them. Each different results should be mandatory explain

Attention! Make the difference between results and conclusions. The results strictly depict the generated overcomes of your analysis, while the conclusions 'cover' the results but in a more profound way. The conclusions comprise economic explanations and interpretations.

5/ The 'Conclusions', not exceeding 1 page, are the last redoubt of your research, very important, chronologically following the 'Results' section.

In the start of the section, you should reiterate the main research objectives, targeted subject, analysed time period, and also the importance of the topic for the literature.

Further, it comes the part where you give explanations and interpretations for the results obtained. Here, never ever appeal at the results or affirmations not demonstrated in the 'Results' section. Please strictly resume at your results!

You cannot have as conclusions your own intuitions and positions related to an economic phenomenon or process.

In the same time, it is a frequent mistake to consider a result as a conclusion. As a consequence, avoid to take as conclusion numbers and analyse generated indicators (e.g. a wrong conclusion is to claim that: 'the main conclusion is that the GDP annually increases with 3.56%').

The section ends with the policy implications of your research, more precisely with your recommendations, from corrective point of view, regarding the fixing of issues targeted by the subject.

Do not forget that a research is useful only if it has a given scope! Therefore, it is required to show how and to whom is necessary your research (e.g. households, companies, governments, NGOs international organisms etc.).

Present here your recommendations to related stakeholders regarding the adequate policies by offering all details about the required measures which allow them to fix the issues treated in the topic.

Certainly, if there are some limits of your approach, do not hesitate to specify them! With the same importance are also the future research directions which you itself propose or suggest to the research community.

The content of comment

The content of comment is generally at the author discretion or can have a structure in three parts:
- introduction;
- demonstration, and
- conclusions.

In this case, the chronology of the parts follows an atypical format from the structural point of view.

1/ The 'Introduction', in contrast to the introduction of the research article, should be a short one, with few phrases. Here, it is required to refer to the commented paper. You can perform a short description of it especially by focusing on the main claimed results. It is not mandatory to offer many details as the interested readers can easily orient toward the published original manuscript.

Try to make comments on the published papers, not on the "working papers". This last category is grounded on unfiltered results, without any specialised review.

2/ The 'Demonstration 'represents the main section of a comment, being the largest part of it. The section debuts with the principal criticism of the results, followed by the motivations and clear identification of the 'weaknesses' which generated the scientific debate. Further, you can continue with the argument which gives sense to your position as all readers, even the original authors of the paper, to understand the criticism and its demonstration. Starting from the criticism, the final part of the section is reserved to the necessary solutions in order to fix the issue identified, where many authors adding future directions of research.

3/ The 'Conclusions' close the comment and resumes, in few words, the main criticism related to the commented paper and the solutions to deal with it. Moreover, you can add also here, in few sentences, any potential future directions of research.

As you can see, the comment is an atypical form of a paper, containing an argued scientific position of a researcher related to already published results.

The content of review

The content of the review is similar to the research paper, with the difference that in this case it does not exist a literature section. Practically, the review has this structure:
- introduction;
- method and data;
- results, and
- discussions and conclusions.

1/ The 'Introduction' is the first section of a review, not more than 2-3 pages, and start with the same 'catch up phrase' as in the case of a research article in order to connect the reader with the importance and opportunity of topic exploration. After that, the next step is to motivate why you choose to investigate the subject, by offering the necessary information (e.g. the argumentations of choosing to review the economic growth models in a country).

Further, you should emphasise the contributions of your research to the literature in the field. Do not forget that the publishing chances increase as your review has major contributions to the literature.

The end of the section is reserved for a short presentation of the review's structure.

2/ The 'Method and data' chronologically follows the 'Introduction' section and has the main goal to offer detailed information related to the selected methodological tool used to analyse the reviewed literature and to describe the dataset.

Do not forget to motivate your methodological choice and to show why your tool is superior to the existing ones used in similar approaches. It is a little bit curious the existence of empirical methods for review, but the literature in field seems to be more than generous in this way.

Frequently, the dataset is a conventional statistical construction, as vector of numerical codification of included papers in review. Herein, different criteria of modelling can be identified, such as: the sub-topic, the subject, the period of investigation and the used methodology. Usually, the data are presented in tabular form, being accompanied by related references as those appear in the body text.

3/ The 'Results' are contoured by the stock of research articles selected for review and follows the 'Methods and data' section, being the essence of this category of papers. Here, there are two directions you should follow: the first one is given by the presentation of the results generated by the interaction between the method and dataset, while the second one is practically a classical literature review similar to the research article but having huge length. The first direction is in reality a statistical approach of targeted literature. The second direction follows the same coordinates as in the case of a research article. Summarizing, the results should contain your own vision about how to analyse a given literature and also your own critical position related to the quality of such literature. Attention! The results are not a number of papers which you identified during the research!

4/ The 'Discussions and conclusions' section gives the essence for the end of a review, being recommended not to exceed 1 page.

Here, you will iterate the main goal of review and the major literature breakpoints identified. Do not forget to highlight your research importance in the given context. Of course, the end of conclusions is attributed to the future research directions, by discussing all the aspects that are not fully clarified in the existing literature or that, why not, yet investigated.

The content of erratum

The content of 'Erratum' is a type of paper at the discretion of author or editor, being focused on any corrections or explanations made to an existing paper, in only one body text.

At the beginning, you will specify all details needed to identify the paper 'subject' of erratum. Further, you will present the main issues identified in the paper, such as estimation errors, text omissions, understanding distortions, typos, misspellings etc. Another aspect is to argue the opportunity of introducing additional explanations by specifying the part of the paper which deserves such adjustments.

Finally, you should offer information regarding the correction of issue and/or the right place for explanations you invoke.

Editing

The editing is the last sequence with you are confronting before giving a final form to your paper. You should not neglect this step as the quality of your manuscript largely depends on also on this stage.

Generally, your manuscript will be edited in an international language, usually in English. This process involves the following two steps:
- the copy-editing, and
- the language editing.

1/ The copy-editing is the first stage of editing a manuscript having the role to give an adequate style from a presentation point of view. The procedure is performed by a specialized person, named copy-editor. Certainly, the copy-editors are specialised on different research domains.

Therefore, if you talk about the economics and business, there are also specialised persons in these domains of the economy.

The copy-editing stage is performed after the full paper is written and has three important steps related to:
- the formatting type;
- the writing style, and
- the text accuracy.

1a/ The formatting type represents the first step of copy-editing procedure which gives a standardized form to the manuscript according to the usual standards which appear in the literature. Here, several details are followed, such as the paper margins, size and the face of fonts for the title page, content, annexes, appendix and also any other details which are connected to the visual image of the paper.

1b/ The writing style refers to all performed paper adjustments regarding the spelling, punctuation, grammar, terminology used, jargon, and also the semantics and syntax.

1c/ The text accuracy is the step in which the copy-editor manages the text in order to ensure a high level of text language as, through reading, to offer an easy and a clear understanding of the results to the interested readers.

Generally, these editing steps of a manuscript are followed for 'research market' test reasons and further for final publication. Attention! It is recommended to think at the publishing step only if you already consumed several mandatory stages at the high research level!

Currently, between the editing stage and the submission stage for publication are also several sequences in which the manuscript has different forms:
- draft paper;
- working paper, and
- final paper version.

i/ The 'draft paper' reveals the manuscript written and filtered through the copy-editing process, having as main destination laboratory seminars, research meetings or research roundtables. As a rule, for such form of paper, below the title of paper appears written the construction 'draft version', where many authors add also the data. The aim of presenting the paper at the small various research events is to disseminate your research results in order to obtain feedbacks from your colleagues, who have similar research interest in the field.

With this occasion, based on the comments, suggestions, observations or, why not, ideas received, you will have the chance to substantially improve your research! Do not be vainglorious and accept that any remarks can increase your paper quality. Additionally, do not forget to insert in "acknowledgements" the names of the persons who gave you their valuable feed-backs.

ii/ The 'working paper' is the second type of edited manuscript and represents the vector of all adjustments made as result of manuscript 'filtering' in the small research events, as you already saw in the previous step.

A very important particularity is given by the fact that the working paper is the first official form of the manuscript, being included and counted in the special working paper series of the big universities, research centres or research organizations (e.g. one of the most famous working paper series is NBER Working Papers[2]). These official series are practically database where are working papers archived. Additionally, these series can offer copyrights

[2] NBER Working Papers is the acronym for National Bureau of Economic Research Working Papers. More details can be obtained by accessing the web address: http://www.nber.org.

protection to the authors.

During the whole period of working paper stage, the manuscript should be 'routinely' presented at different congresses, conferences, symposiums or any other research events, national or international. Preferably is to focus on the events having the same topic as the paper. In this case, the objective is to receive new feed-backs, which allow you to improve the quality of your research.

iii/ The 'final paper version' is in reality an updated version of a working paper, resulted following the adjustments performed according to the feed-backs received at congresses, conferences, symposiums or any other research events.

2/ The language-editing is the second step of copy-editing procedure and refers to the checking and correction of a paper written in an international language. For example, if the paper is written in English, the procedure is called English-editing. Here, it is obviously understood that the article, before to be language-edited, it should be translated (is easily to write directly the paper in the targeted language).

The language-editing is performed by specialised

persons in such services (eng. language-editor), who are native speakers, with significant experience in the considered research domain.

Irrespective of circumstances do not try to 'fix' this step by calling for corrections performed by non-native speakers and non-specialized persons in the domain! Should you opt for a non-specialised language editing, the decision of any recognized publisher will be an unpleasant surprise, consisting in the rejection of you paper. Many times, for the paper written in foreign languages, the two stages of editing (i.e. the copy-editing and the language editing) are overlapped.

As soon as the paper is finished, its final version, irrespective of the targeted language, can be prepared for submission in order to be considered for publication in different specialized journals.

Publishing

The publishing represents the crowning success of your research activity. Through publshing you make known your findings and, in the same time, allows you to increase both your visibility and scientific notoriety as a researcher.

There are three aspects which I consider essential to be known in the publishing process:
- the journal selection;
- the publishing stages, and
- the publishing announcement.

The journal selection

The understanding all the aspects related to the journal selection represents a crucial aspect which has the capacity to maximize the chance of publication. Only with a very good publishing strategy you can achieve the expected effects.

Not considering them as rules, several sequences are recommended to be followed in the journal targeting:
- the identification of the journals which have as declared topic your topic, and
- the withdrawing of the 'fake' journals.

1/ The identification of the journals which have as declared topic your topic is not a difficult process and can be made by accessing indexed international databases. Very useful are here ISI Thomson Web of Science and Scopus. Please, do not confuse the acronym ISI Thomson powered by Reuters® with that claimed by doubtful databases, with short form 'ISI'. In the same time, you can access similar online platforms or publishers online systems, which offer to the readers papers of very good quality (e.g. ScienceDirect, Springer, Jstore, Taylor & Francis, Sage, Emerald etc.).

A major part of them allow the readers to use different forms of searching: by domains, by sub-domains or by keynotes and JEL codes.

Even if the journals are found in the ISI Thomson

database, take yourself several precaution measures and avoid the journals which:

- have high fees for submission and publication (more than 150 Euro);
- publish authors who abound in self-citations or cite generally only certain journals (the cites are called cross-citations and have as main objective the increase of journal's impact factor);
- publish papers also from other domains than those declared in title and journal aim;
- are not specialized (you can target also multidisciplinary journals but you must be careful at the quality of editors), or
- publish many papers per issue, with many co-authors per paper (i.e. more than 4-5 co-authors).

A major part of these journals will be, sooner or later, penalized by Thomson Reuters and in this way you can lose very important points in your professional image.

If you still have the preference for less recognized publishers, you should be sure that the journals found, on internet, with any searching engine, offer a minimal quality of published papers.

Avoid journals which:
- are not specialized (you can consider also

multidisciplinary journals but you should take into account the quality of the editors);
- promise short period of publication;
- invoke different types of indexing which are not genuine (it is preferably to check the validity of indexing and to take care of the journals strictly declared 'ISI'),
- have high submission or publishing fees (e.g. more than 150 Euro);
- claim an editorial board with major part of members by the same nationality or with a very extended structure;
- publish papers having the majority authors of the same nationality;
- do not have editors with a good and recognized professional reputation (you can easily check this status, based on the CV and list of publications available on internet);
- have editors who are not visible on internet at all;
- are affiliated to some modest universities or research organisms;
- abound in special issues;
- are related to the conferences with high frequency of organization, in different world places and 'rich' social programmes;
- do not have an ISSN and/or miss the classical identification elements (aim, editorial board,

instructions for authors, information for reviewers, contact address, indexing status, publication ethic rules etc.);

- publish papers also from other domains than those declared in title and aim;

- have authors who excel in self-citations and cite generally certain journals (i.e. these cross-citations have as main scope to increase the impact factor of the journal);

- have 'luxuriant' websites from visual point of view, and

- publish a high number of papers per issue, with many co-authors per paper (i.e. more than 4-5 co-authors).

Finally, another tip to select the targeted journal is to focus on the journals where are published authors cited by you in your paper references list. In many cases, this criterion can be a very good one.

2/ The withdrawing of the 'fake' journals is the last sequence in the journal selection through you should check in which measure the targeted journals are or not genuine journals.

The reality is the fact that, over the last years, as a result of the internet development, several journals, generally prestigious ones, have fallen victims of illegal practices, being so called 'hijacked' journals. The practice means that the official journals are replicated by different pirate websites.

The promoted journals there are realized in 'mirror' with the genuine ones, being in fact cheats, which have as scope to financially fraud the naive potential authors. Therefore, all such journals exist in reality, are authentic, but have a 'stepsister' who are 'badly' interested.

OK! How can you make a distinction between the genuine and fake journals? Even if the differences can be identified with difficulty, there are several aspects which are better to be considered:
- the journals do not belong to recognized editors;
- the journals are managed by universities and prestigious research organisms;
- the journal appears, usually, only in the 'print' format;
- the journals are usually indexed by ISI Thomson;
- there is not any correspondence between the indexed ISI Thomson published papers and those published in the suspected journal;
- the editorial board of pirated version comprises persons who either do not exist in reality or

belong to different research domains;
- in the case of fake journals, the decision of publication accepting is given in only few days, or
- the required fees for submission, publication or reading access at the fake journal are huge.

The international experience reveals at least three famouse cases of recognized journals which became 'victims' of such practices. From professional deontological reasons and to discourage such illegal practices, I will present below three famous cases:

- 'Wulfenia' journal : with genuine website address at "http://www.landesmuseum.ktn.gv.at/210226w_DE.htm?seite=15", and with the 'hijacked' one at "http://www.multidisciplinarywulfenia.org/";

- 'Jökull' journal: with genuine website address at "http://jokulljournal.is", and with the 'hijacked' one at "http://www.jokulljournal.com", as well as

- 'Archives des sciences' journal: with genuine website address at "http://www.unige.ch/sphn/" and with the 'hijacked' one at "http://www.archiveofscience.com/".

After you selected the targeted journals, the next step is to choose one of them for publishing. If you do not have a good publishing experience, it is recommended to 'attack' in a first stage journals with modest qualitative works and further to orient to journals with high rankings.

The publishing stages

After you selected the journal targeted for publishing, a very important stage is the managing of the relationship quality with the journal editorial board. Frequently ignored by many authors, the way of how we communicate with the journal is also very important, maybe crucial, in the publishing process.

Concretely, there are 7 stages which a manuscript should follow, from the submission stage until the stage of effective publication, sure in the case when everything will be fine:
- the stage "with journal";
- the stage "with editor";
- the stage "under review";
- the stage "under revision";
- the stage "awaiting editorial decision";
- the stage "under publishing process", and
- the stage "published".

If your manuscript does not have the quality to be accepted for publication, then the status 'rejected' arises already in the stage 'with editor' or, more frustrating, in the stages 'under review' or 'under revision'.

1/ The stage 'with journal' is the first sequence in the publishing process. Concretely, in this case, you should prepare your manuscript according to the journal criteria and, after that, to submit the formatted manuscript.

Pay a special attention and respect the professional conduct and ethical rules in publishing, which either are clearly declared in a journal or are generally accepted at the international level.[3] If you send already published papers, papers in the process of publication or manuscript already submitted to other journals, your professional career at the international level is over! More serious are the cases of plagiarism and self-plagiarism![4] The majority of publishers and international

---

[3] For more details, please access the webpage of the Committee on Publication Ethics (COPE), at http://publicationethics.org.

[4] A good explanation of the phenomenon is given by Oxford University at https://www.ox.ac.uk/students/academic/guidance/skills/plagiarism?wssl=1.

organizations in the field keep fighting against such unorthodox practices![5] Unfortunately, there are countries which hold top positions in respect to the number of detected and demonstrated cases of plagiarism at the international level.

The whole instructions regarding the manuscript preparation are specified by the journal within the rubric 'guide for authors'. All those criteria must be fully respected, any exceptions generating the paper rejection. Many current journals have online platforms which facilitate both the editors and authors works.

A special attention should be paid to the manuscript submission process, which generally includes several components (i.e. electronic files, for the journals with publishing online platform): the letter to editor, the manuscript without the names of authors (so-called 'blank manuscript'), the title page and also any other supplementary materials, if appropriate.

The letter to the editor is a document where the author addresses to the editor of the journal, informing about the submission of the manuscript. You should specify the names of all co-authors (if the case), the title of paper, the aim

---

[5] See, for example, https://plagiarism.repec.org.

of research as well as the main obtained overcomes. Certainly, at the end of the letter, do not forget to thank by using a very polite language.

As soon as above documents were prepared, if the journal has an online interface, the submission can be made by using the option 'submit your paper/submit online' or by sending the manuscript directly to the editor. In the second case, some journals receive the papers through an email address, while others prefer the old procedure, by using the post services (i.e. the paper is sent in hard-copy).

Not at least, it is required to check carefully the financial conditions of publishing as many journals are practicing fees for submission of final publication.

2/ The stage 'with editor' follows the stage 'with journal' and represents a sequence where the editor made the first reading of the manuscript. If the manuscript has potential, the editor will decide either to send it to referees for review or to assign another editor, called associate editor. The associate editor, who is more specialized in the paper topic, will also read the paper and send it to referee for review, if appropriate.

If the paper is not in the journal interest or has poor quality, then it will be rejected. However, it is not a guaranty for publication even if the paper is sent to referees.

When your research is absolutely remarkable, it may happen, in rare case, that the editor decides the publication of your paper even in this stage. Usually, this is called "publication from editor".

3/ The stage 'under review' generally takes between 6 and 12 months, when the paper is analyzed and assessed by 1 to 3 referees assigned by the editorial board. Each referee will perform a review report where will offer a personal point of view regarding the opportunity of publishing the paper, the resolution being:
- accepted for publication;
- accepted for publication with minor revision;
- accepted for publication with moderate revision;
- accepted for publication with major revision;
- reject and resubmit, and
- rejected.

As soon as the review reports have been sent to the journal, based on the resolutions offered by referees, the editor or associate editor will decide if the manuscript will be published (here the stage is "awaiting editor decision"), will be sent for revision or will be rejected.

For the manuscripts accepted for revision, the authors will receive from editor all needed referee reports/review reports.

4/ The stage 'under revision' is in fact a period of time when the author should respond and adjust the research according to the referees recommendations. It is crucial to offer feed-backs to all referees comments and, very important, to avoid inutile polemics, even if the comments are exaggerated or impossible to be fixed. In all circumstances do not use an licentious language, which is strictly forbidden.

After you finish the revision, the revised paper should be submitted to journal on term and will have the following documents: a letter to editor where you thank for the opportunity to revise the paper, letters to referees with clear information about how you fixed all their comments and suggestions as well as, sure, the revised manuscript.

5/ The stage 'awaiting editor decision' is a step where the editor or associate editor will send the revised manuscript to the same referees in order to see if they accept or not the responses of authors and related adjustments. After the feed-backs of referees, the editor will decide if the paper will be publish or not. Sometime here it is possible that the decision to be in the favour of a new revision (practically is the second revision), and the cycle of publishing reiterates.

6/ The stage 'under publishing process' is one of professional accomplishment and comes on the ground of paper publishing acceptance, given by the editor in the previous stage.

The main work here is a technical one and is called "handling". Under 'handling' a specialist person assigned by the publisher will 'arrange' the paper in the final publication form. The resulting product of handling process is called 'proof' and represents the paper adjusted according to the journal's publication criteria. Please note that the 'proof' also needs to be revised by the author, being the last time when he interact with the paper before publication. After checking, the 'proof' will become final article, already prepared for effective publication.

Please do not neglect the fact that many journals have fees for publication, which should be paid after the paper is accepted for publication.

7/ The stage 'published' is the last sequence of

publishing process, when the article appears, in the first instance, online and after that in print form. Many times, certain journals, before effective publication, posts the article in online form. In such situations, the article has attached a cover and identification details (i.e. so called digital object identifier, known under acronym „DOI"[6]), but does not have allocated year, volume, issue and page numbers. As soon as the article has been published, its results should be announced on the economic research environment in order to be known by the interested readers.

The publication announcement

After the publication of article, the last auhtor's effort is related to the promotion of the results as the whole scientific community to take note of them.

This step should not be neglected because the increase of your publication visibility allows you to maximize the numbers of citations, makes you known and, why not, ensures you good perspectives for further collaborations. Not at

---

[6] For details please consult http://www.doi.org.

least, the publication can be a good starting point for identifying of new research directions.

Generally, the publication announcement will be made by the editor of the journal, on the journal's online platform or in its content, such practice being widely used in the world.

However, it is not an effort to announce the publication by yourself, through an email sent to all your colleagues. In the email, specify the paper title, the topic and the main obtained findings as well as all needed details regarding the journal where you published: the journal name, the volume, issue and the pages. Certainly, if the article appears only in electronic form, as "open access", you can attach the paper and also send the link, accordingly. If your article is not an "open access" and the copyrights were transferred to the publisher, irrespective of the circumstances do not send to your colleagues the electronic form or scanned version of the paper, because you risk being involved in conflicts of interest with the publisher.

Another way to increase your article's visibility is to post all the above mentioned details on your personal or professional webpage. Do not forget about the restrictions regarding the access to the content of the article. Lastly, more and more researchers started to promote their works also on professional and social online networks.

References

https://www.aeaweb.org/econlit/jelCodes.php

http://www.doi.org

http://www.nber.org.

https://plagiarism.repec.org.

http://publicationethics.org.

https://www.ox.ac.uk/students/academic/guidance/skills/plagiarism?wssl=1.

About author

Mihai Mutascu is a full professor of public economics at the Faculty of Economics and Business Administration, from West University of Timisoara, and associate researcher at the Laboratory of Economics of Orleans (LEO), from University of Orleans.

He published many papers in recognized international journals, such as: International Review of Economics & Finance, Empirical Economics, Energy Economics, Economic Modelling, Renewable & Sustainable Energy Reviews, Journal of Economic Policy Reform, Journal of Applied Economics and Business Research, European Economics Letters, Management of Environmental Quality: An International Journal, Review of Economic Perspectives, Contemporary Economics, Economics Bulletin, Analisis Politico, Empirical Economics Letter or Economic Analysis and Policy.

Starting with 2011, Mihai is Editor-in-Chief of the journal 'Economic Research Guardian'.